Poetic Inspirations

by

David Jacque

David J

To: Pastor M. E. Gaston

10/10/04

POETIC INSPIRATIONS

First Edition 1998

Second Edition 2002

Scripture quotations have been taken from the King James version of the Bible and the Zondervan New International version.

To contact the author write:
David Jacque
P O Box 618
Dimondale, Michigan 48821
Email: ministerjd@yahoo.com

Poetic Inspirations / David Jacque
ISBN 976-8160-54-3

ACKNOWLEDGMENTS

Thanks to God who has given me the strength and the unction to write this book and the patience to endure the hardships of life and remain in His will. I am very grateful for the companions of my soul goodness and mercy which follows me every where I go.

Traci Jacque a remarkable woman of God, my wife and the mother of my children.

April, Jessica, Jasmyne my daughters and my son Josiah which will be born Spring 2002.

Professor Bethanye Bagby

Dr. Phyllis Brathwaite

Pastor Bertril Baird

CONTENTS

CHAPTER		PAGE #
	Foreword	8
I.	LOVING RELATIONSHIPS	11
	True Friends	12
	Love thy neighbor	13
	How much I care	14
	America Arise	15
II.	GOD'S FAMILY DESIGN	17
	The Family	18
	Husbands love your wives	19
	Appreciation to Father	20
	Appreciation of Mother	21
	Divorce	22
III.	APPRECIATING GOD'S LOVE	23
	God is...	24
	Who is Jesus?	26
	Holy Ghost within	27
	What kind of man is this?	28

IV.	GODLY CONVERSATIONS	31
	Lord Why?	32
	The Altar	33
	Intercessors	34
	Cries in the inner city	35
	What can we do?	36
	The Gospel Train	37
V.	No More Wrong Stuff	39
	Trouble	40
	A cry for life	41
	Holiness or Hell	42
	Be Prepared	43
	Be not deceived	44
	A deceitful heart	45
VI.	WE WILL STAND	47
	The Race	48
	Why we suffer?	49
	Lord make me real	50
	Green Grass	51
	This is war	52

VII. We are getting better 55

Forgive 56
Reconciliation is God's plan 57
Watch your words 59
I can change 60
Watch what you think 62
Pray 63

VIII. Building each Other 65

I believe in you 66
The Inspirators 67
He is with you 68
My Child 69
You believe in me 70

IX. Blessed Assurances 71

Jesus Comforts 72
The last shall be first 74
His Glory 75
I believe God 76

X. Helping Hands 77

A Champion for the masses 78
Give 79
Prayer Partners 80
I owe you 81

XI. All in a Day 83

You are different 84
Tell the truth about Christmas 85
I am a Christian 86
Laughter 87
Death 88
I have a home in glory 89

About the Author 90

FOREWORD

"The pen is mightier than the sword." These words are truer than they seem, for it is the power of the pen that have captivated the hearts and imaginations of generations through literary works that tell our story.

Throughout history man's life, tragedy, fear, mysteries, and the unknown have been captured in oral tradition and the written word for generations afterward to appreciate and enjoy. Many have used the pen to express their emotions, aspirations, and sediments for others to identify with. No other form of literary expression has accomplished this more effectively than the pen of the poet. It is said that history lives in the pages of the pen.

No other emotion has captured the imagination of the heart of man like the common experience we all have in life expressed in poetry and prose. **"Poetic Inspirations"** is such a work and will be cherished in history as a masterpiece of poetry and prose genius. David Jacque has captured the spirit, emotion, beauty, and moods of the human experience in a way that cause you to transcend the shallows of life, and transport you to the depths of the human spirit. His graphic descriptions, cultural antidotes, and familiar emotional experiences buried within each page will give the reader a variety of emotional experiences. A smile, a tear, and laughter are only some of the emotions to be stirred by these words crafted by the artist of the pen. I encourage you to read on and enjoy. **"Poetic Inspirations"** and experience the journey through the land of life while inspiring you to live a fuller life.

Dr. Myles Munroe
Bahamas Faith Ministries International
Nassau, Bahamas

CHAPTER I

LOVING RELATIONSHIPS

- TRUE FRIENDS
- LOVE THY NEIGHBOR
- HOW MUCH I CARE
- AMERICA ARISE

TRUE FRIENDS

Though I speak with the voices of men and of angels and
have no friends,
I am become as a sounding brass or a tingling cymbal.

And though I have the gift of prophecy,
And understand all mysteries, and all knowledge,

And though I have all faith, so that I could remove
mountains, and have no friends,
I am nothing.

And though I give all my goods to feed the poor,
And though I give my body to be burned, and have no
friends, I gain nothing.

Friends suffer long and are kind; friends do not envy,
Friends do not brag or boast on themselves they are not
puffed up.

Friends do not behave themselves unseemly, do not
seek their own,
Are not easily provoked, think no evil.

Friends do not rejoice in iniquity, but rejoice in the truth,
Friends bear all things, believe all things.

Hope all things, endure all things.
True friends, like true love, will never end.

"Greater love hath no man than this, that a man will lay down his life for his friends." St. John 15:13

Love Thy Neighbor

Love my neighbor as myself, the preacher said
I don't know why? Neighbors can give you hell.

They do not speak and neither do I,
But we acknowledge each other with gestures as we go by.

Most Sunday mornings, we head to our churches,
Going to God with our praise and worship.

We will drive past you as though you were a post.
Better not get stranded on your way to church.

If Jesus needed a ride while we were on our way.
"Too bad for you," I believe many Christians would say.

And you better not be broke and ask at the church,
Some will flatly tell you, "you need to work."

Others will reply, "I can help you."
While some say, "have faith in God, he will bless you."

So if you are a Christian be real, don't bc a fake,
Love your neighbor and share, it is part of being in the faith.

"As you would that men should do to you, ye also do them likewise." Luke 6:31

HOW MUCH I CARE

How much I fear to share, I care for you
To allow my heart to tell exactly how it feels about you.

How much I long to express what you are to me.
You are more than a friend, and all other company.

How much longer should I wait and anticipate, to express,
These heart throb expressions that rest within my breast.

I yearn to tell you I care, but I fear to share,
I am in despair; can you see how much I care

"But I rejoiced in the Lord greatly, that now at last your care of me hath flourished again; wherein ye were also careful, but ye lacked opportunity." Phil. 4: 10

America Arise

America arise
Wipe the tears from your eyes
Allow the Lord to take the sighs
And place upon your face a smile

America I heard your cry
The sound of your wailing could not go by
I felt your pain the enemy inflicted
If you trust me I will soon repay him

America I see the blow
From the air the enemy struck down below
The World Trade Center and thousand of lives
The enemy claimed for a prize

America remember me
For only in me you can have victory
Put me last and they shall prevail
If I am first, then you will be the head and not the tail

America what will it be?
Will I be your God or will you bow to the enemy?
Make me your God and you will see
I will destroy your enemies

America my children bow down to me
For I am the Lord God Almighty
Bend your knees and pray to me
And you will rise and destroy this enemy

America I comfort thee
My hands are out stretch with grace and mercy
I counsel thee to lean on me
For I am you God Almighty

"Oh that I were as in times past, as in the days when God preserved me. When his candle shined upon my head, and when by his light I walked through darkness. As I was in the days of my youth, when the secret of God was upon my tabernacle."
Job 29: 2-4

CHAPTER II

GOD'S FAMILY DESIGN

- THE FAMILY
- HUSBAND LOVE YOUR WIVES
- APPRECIATION TO FATHER
- APPRECIATION TO MOTHER
- DIVORCED

The Family

The family is ordained of God designed with a husband and
a wife.
God set the order for the family, male with female to birth life

He gave the authority to the man
Rule, provide and love your wife was God's command.

Some wives disagree
Rebelling against their husbands and God's authority.

Mad with God for making man their head
These wives claim to have equal authority instead.

Not submitting and obeying their husbands
They believe its wrong for them to be in subjection.

Astonishing, as it may seem, the devil had the same mentality
He refused to submit to God's authority.

Wives if you have a problem with your husbands
Don't argue or fight make your appeal to Christ.

For Christ is the head of the man
And the man is the head of the woman

"Wives submit yourselves unto your own husbands, as unto the Lord. For the husband is the head of the wife, even as Christ is the head of the church; and he is the savior of the body." Ephesians 5: 22-23

Husband Love your Wives

Man do you take this woman to be your wife
To love and to cherish
In sickness and in health
In good times and bad until death do you part?

I do!
I now pronounce you husband and wife.

I know I am the head of my wife
And God has charged me to treat her nice.
I am not her king to rule her life.
I am a husband that loves my wife.

We have forsaken all for each other,
Father, mother, sisters and brothers.
No longer twain we are one and the same
With my wife bearing my name.

Cherishing and honoring her is my responsibility.
Communicating with her shows respect in our family.
Though I am the head and have the God given authority.
I submit myself to my wife and listen to her attentively.
Its all a part of being nice and shows a husband loves his wife

"Husbands love your wives, even as Christ also loved the church and gave himself for it." Ephesians 5: 25

Appreciation to Father

Father, you are a very special person.
There is not another like you this side of heaven.
You are a man of integrity and character,
And you are an excellent provider.

You watched over the home with love and care.
Father I commend you for always being there.
The money you made did not make you great.
It was the times together and the support you gave.

Father, you are my champion
And a wonderful example of a man.
You communicated so many wonderful things,
And proved your love for your family time and time again.

You did not leave me to raise myself.
But were there to instruct and offer help.
Not once did you compromise on my upbringing,
Even when you had to do the painful thing and discipline.

Thank you dad for being a good father.
You have shown me the love of our Heavenly Father.

"And ye fathers, provoke not your children to wrath: but bring them up in the nurture and admonition of the Lord."
Ephesians 6: 4

APPRECIATION TO MOTHER

Mother you are like no other
I am thankful you are my mother, not a sister or brother.
You were born to be my mother chosen of God.
To birthed me into this world.

The life you lived before me is a life sanctify and holy.
You demonstrated by bowing your knees every morning
And spending time with Jesus before the day's dawning,
And every evening you gathered us together to read the scripture.

Mother you are worth more than rubies
Denying your needs and desires to provide for your family.
I realize the sacrifice you made just for me.
When I think of how you gave so unselfishly.

You were remarkably, kind and wise.
Ministering also to the needs of your neighbors.
You were excellent in providing for our home
And your family loves you and thank you for a wonderful home.

"Who can find a virtuous woman? For her price is far above rubies. The heart of her husband doth safely trust in her, so that he shall have no need of spoil. Her children rise up and call her blessed; her husband also and he praiseth her."
Proverb 31: 10-11, 28

Divorced

I never ever thought it could happen to me.
Who me? I will never be a divorcee.

This is not going to happen in my relationship,
And that's one club I don't wish to have a membership.

There is nothing nice about a divorce.
Regardless who is right or wrong the marriage is loss

You never could imagine the agony
That divorce puts upon a family.

It destroys and leaves crying,
Two hearts fatally wounded and dying.

The pain from the separation is so severe
It seems almost too much to bear.

Dejected all strength is gone
Angry and disappointed I nurse my wounds.

As I rehearsed what went wrong in my heart.
I realize that divorce like death, rips one apart.

Thank you Lord for forgiveness and grace
Let this poem help someone from becoming a divorce case.

"What therefore God had joined together let no man put asunder." Mark 10: 9

CHAPTER III

APPRECIATING GOD'S LOVE

- GOD IS...
- WHO IS JESUS?
- HOLY GHOST WITHIN
- WHAT KIND OF MAN IS THIS?

God is...

He is Alpha and Omega.
He is the beginning of everything.
In the beginning God, created everything, the heaven and earth.
He spoke and there was light,
And the gathering together of the waters he called seas.

He is our provider.
He provided the earth with grass, herbs with herb bearing seeds,
And fruit trees bearing fruit with seed after their kind.
And God gave every herb and fruit bearing seed for meat.

God is the husbandman
He spoke and the waters brought forth the creatures that had life.
And He created great whales, and all the creatures that the water brought forth.
And he blessed them saying, be fruitful and multiply, fill the waters in the seas, and fowls multiply in the earth.
And let the earth bring forth the living creature after its kind, the cattle after their kind and the beast after his kind.
And everything that crept upon the earth after his kind and God saw that it was good.

God is our Father
And our Father said let us make man in our own image, and after our likeness.
So he created man, in His own image, in the image of God he created them male and female.
And the Father blessed them saying, be fruitful and multiply and replenish the earth, and subdue it.

God the Father created all things, and everything he made was very good, and they all came from Him.

He is Alpha and Omega, the beginning of everything and He is the end of all things.

"In the beginning God created the heaven and the earth."
Genesis 1: 1

Who is Jesus?

Jesus is the Christ, the Son of the living God
He is the Messiah, which is Christ the anointed One
He is the Word, that was made flesh and dwelt among us.
He is our Lord and Master
He is Emmanuel, God with us.

Who is Jesus?
Jesus is the bread of life that came down from Heaven.
He is the Light of the world, which shines in darkness,
And the darkness cannot comprehend the Light.
He is the Resurrection and the life, he that believe on him
Though he is dead shall live again.

So who is Jesus?
He is the true vine and we are the branches.
He is our High Priest that offered Himself for our sins.
He is our Mediator before God.
He is our Intercessor for He makes intercession for us.
He is our advocate, pleading for us before the Father when we sin
He is the Lamb of God that took away the sin of the world.
Jesus is the beginner and finisher of our faith.

"I am the Alpha and Omega, the beginning and the ending, said the Lord, which is, and which is to come, the Almighty."
Revelation 1: 8

Holy Ghost Within

Lord fill us with the Holy Ghost
It is your Spirit Lord we thirst
You sent him to be our Comforter
And fill the longing in our souls

Take your place in us Holy Spirit
We welcome you into our lives.
Lead and guide and teach our spirit
How to follow you, the Guide

You give no respect to persons
And fills the longing in every soul
You are the God in the earth today
Working mightily through men of clay.

So speak to us daily Holy Spirit
As we travel this holy way.
Bring the word to our remembrance
As we walk along the way.

Holy Spirit, abide in us daily.
Satisfy the thirsting of our souls,
Make our hearts to know joy and gladness
That comes from obeying the Spirit and the word.

"But the comforter which is the Holy Ghost, whom the Father will send in my name, He shall teach you all things, and all things to your remembrance whatsoever I have said unto you."
St. John 14: 26

What Kind of Man is this?

That will leave his home in glory
And come to earth to die for humanity
This is not a natural man
For no man could of manufacture such a master plan

That will redeem man from the enemy hand
Except it is the Son of Man
Who was from the beginning of time
Clothed himself in humanity though he was divine

He is the one that created man
And gave them His command
For man's sins He paid the ultimate penalty
And His life He gave to set them free

This is not superman
That was a character of the human mind
But this is the Christ man, very God very man
He opened the eyes of the blind

He healed the sick and raise the dead
Over five thousand he fed
With two fishes and five loaves of bread
This was a miracle to beheld

The Christ man is not carnal He is divine
He is God's plan to save mankind
He lived here till He was thirty three
Then they took him to Calvary

Crucified Him there for you and me
And his enemies thought he was history
Because the Son of Man was buried in a cemetery
But God gave Him the victory

To their amazement the third day He rose
Proclaiming victory over death, hell and all his foes
And through His resurrection we have hope
If we accept the savior death, resurrection and birth

Though some will never accept His divinity
In Him we have life for eternity
And victory over sin and our enemy
For truly He is Jesus Christ which gave us the victory

"For there is one God, and one mediator between God and man, the man Christ Jesus." 1Timothy 2: 5

Chapter IV

Godly Conversations

- Lord Why?
- The Altar
- Intercessors
- Cries in the inner City
- What can we do?
- The Gospel Train

LORD WHY?

Lord, why are men rejecting you?
What have you done, that cause men to refuse you?

You gave your life, laid down your royal diadem,
Just to restore man into God's divine plan.

I thought since you died for man,
That surely man would understand.

Lord, what is man complaint that he is holding against you?
That, few choose your side and few yet live for you.

Some will even die than surrender their lives to you.
While others chose to be a slave to sin than receive you.

Why Lord, why is it that men do not want you?
What have you done to turn them against you?

You died to set men free is this how he chooses to repay you?
Lord you gave your life as a sacrifice, and man still rejects you.

Lord I thank you, that by your grace, I am one of the few,
That accepted your offer to follow you.

"Then said Jesus unto His disciples, if any man will come after me let him deny himself, and take up his cross, and follow mw."
Matthew 16: 24

The Altar

Oh, how I long for the altar
A place of conspicuous surrender
The place where the saints shed their tears
As they lay it all on the altar

Many of the saints lay before God there
As they pray and cry for God to deliver
Sons and daughters, mothers and fathers
Receive deliverance through the altar

Over time things have changed,
With a generation that does not know the importance of the altar.
They have substituted praise for prayer,
For the times we spent before God at the altar.

Oh, how I long for the altar
A place of conspicuous surrender
A place where we give God our body and soul
As we lay our all on the altar

The altar is the saints' hospital
And it is there that we speak to our lawyer
The Glory of the Lord always meets us there
And it is there that we are healed and delivered
Oh, how I long for the altar

"And another angel came and stood at the altar, having a golden censer; and there was given unto him much incense, that he should offer it with the prayers of all saints upon the golden altar which was before the throne." Revelation 8: 3

Intercessors

Lord is there no intercessors in the land?
Is there no one to intercede on the behalf of man?
Lord what happened to the days of old?
When the saints would shut in, within the church.

All night long they prayed seeking your face.
Interceding for men, that God will have mercy and grace.
Lord intercessors are vanishing from within the body.
You are calling them home, while many others would not pray.

Holy Spirit teach the young to intercede, so there are intercessors
in our day.
For even you the Bible states, makes intercession for the saints.
There is such an outward show in the church today.
Many are praising but few are willing to pray.

Dancing and shouting, they do not know what about.
They exhibit no power that will cast the devil out.
Lord you live forever to make intercession for the saints.
Help us I pray, that we will be intercessors once again.

"And he saw that there was no man, and wondered that there was no intercessor, therefore his arm brought salvation unto him, and his righteousness, it sustained him." Isaiah 59: 16

Cries in the Inner City

Help me come the cry from the inner city some call the hood.
Somebody help me is their cry,
From the people throughout these neighborhoods

As I walk through the streets, where few Christians go,
I see churches have moved out, into the suburbs.
Taking with them the message of salvation as they go.

You left us to be the light of the world and the salt of the earth.
But many have left their calling,
Ministering to those that already know.

It seems no one wants to proclaim the gospel in these places.
But if Jesus were to walk the earth again,
We would find him healing and teaching in these very places.

In His word, He left us examples and commandments
And sent the Holy Ghost, so we can witness throughout the land.
His message to every believer is go into every area of the world,
And into the inner cities where people are dying without the word

"Then said he unto his disciples, the harvest truly is plenteous, but the laborers are few; pray ye therefore the Lord of the harvest, that he will send forth laborers into his harvest."
Matthew 9: 37-38

WHAT CAN WE DO?

Now that we are saved, tell me
What can we do?
Or what will you do?
With this new life Christ has given you

How can you repay Him?
For the insults and the beatings
Tell me, just what will you give Him
For the crown of thorns they put upon Him

What will you say to Him?
When you look into His eyes
And see the scars in His hands and feet
And where they pierced Him in the side

Just what will you give?
For his crucifixion on Calvary
For the time He spent on the cross must have seem like eternity
But, He stayed there just for you and me

What words of comfort can be spoken?
Or what great deeds can be done?
To compensate our Savior
For the days he spent in the middle of the ground.

"What shall I render unto the Lord for all his benefits towards me? I will take the cup of salvation, and call upon the name of the Lord." Psalm 116: 12-13

The Gospel Train

What is this I see?
That stretches across land and seas
Is this the Gospel Train?
To ride you must be born again

There are so many aboard
And still there seem to be room for more.
I wonder if it will stop for me?
I cried out Lord have mercy please.

He forgave me of all my sins
And gave me a new life aboard the train
He led me to a car
And placed me under a pastor

On the Gospel Train I learn
The train was heading to its heavenly home
The driver knew the way
For it was him that came on Pentecost day

I could not hide my joy
Spiritually I was just a boy
I thank God for the Gospel Train
And for being born again.

All aboard I heard in the spirit
The call to board and be eternally lifted
I started for my heavenly home that day
As the Holy Spirit led the way

"In the year that King Uzziah died I saw also the Lord sitting upon a throne, high and lifted up, and his train filled the temple." Isaiah 6: 1

Chapter V

No More Wrong Stuff

Trouble

A Cry for Life

Holiness or Hell

Be Prepared

Be not deceived

A deceitful Heart

Trouble

Trouble has no respect of persons
And it does not discriminate.

It knocks at the door of every one's life
And if it gets in, it brings confusion and strife.

It comes when you least expect
And always stays longer if you let it.

It brings nothing good when it appears on the scene
Heartache and turmoil can always be seen

It strives on confusion
And delights in seeing us stressed

Sometimes it brings out the worst in us
When it should be our very best.

It will destroy homes, and separate families
End friendships and turn brothers into enemies.

Trouble can work for your good
If you pray and stay in the right mood
For regardless of how long trouble last
It too will past.

"For we know that all things work together for the good, to them that love the Lord, and are called according to his purpose."
Romans 8: 28

A Cry for Life

Mother, please mother, please let me live.
Give me a chance to grow up and get real big.

Mother I know it was not your plan to have me at this time.
But please mother, please do not abort me, you will be fine.

Can you feel me growing inside you mother?
I am your baby, mother. I am alive.

So why abort me and live with the guilt for the rest of your life.
When you can be proud to have your beautiful baby at your side?

Today you are carrying me, but this will not always be.
Just wait a while and you will see.

Give me a chance, mother. Please let me live.
It is my life you are aborting I am not a twig.

Mother please stop, don't destroy me, don't kill me, stop!
Mother help! Tell the doctor to stop, help he is ripping me out.

I could have been the future President of this Country
Or the scientist, that discovered the cure for AIDS.

So please mother please, reconsider before you terminate me.
All I am asking for is a chance to live.

"The thief cometh not, but for to steal and to kill, and to destroy. I am come that they might have life, and they might have it more abundantly." St. John 10: 10

Holiness or Hell

Once upon a time not so long ago
The fear of God was preached by every man of God you know.
They preached with such conviction concerning the penalty of sin
And the reality of an angry God that will burn up everything.

It has been said, they preached brimstone and fire
The wrath of God to be poured out on the earth
Crying repent, repent and live holy, save your souls
Partake not of the evil that is in this world.

They men and women it is holiness or hell
Stating emphatically, if you are not saved
You are on your way to hell.

They seized every opportunity to stand up for the Lord
Boldly proclaiming "Holiness or Hell" from the word of God.
The message was so profound many surrendered and did not run
And gave their lives to Jesus, for Him to turn their lives around.

Their favorite text "Follow peace with all men,
And holiness, without which no man shall see the Lord"

They believed it and lived it, and taught it very well.
It is God's will that men live holy or spend eternity in hell.

"And that ye put on the new man, which after God is created in righteousness and true holiness." Ephesians 4: 24

Be Prepared

What is this I hear
The church is not going to be here
No one is prepared if Jesus should tarry there.

Some try hard to prove their view
That Christ will rapture you
Before the tribulations of those days come true

While others will say
The church will be here during those days
And the tribulation shall be a time of dismay

When tribulation is on every hand
The church cannot understand
We were not prepared to be a part of the suffering in the land.

If the Lord does not shorten the days
The very elect shall not be saved
Oh! What a terrible day, wouldn't say.

I exhort you to be prepared
If the Lord should tarry there
And the tribulation is here and everywhere.

No time to prove who is right or wrong
Pray God help you to be strong
And you are ready upon Christ's return.

"Immediately after the tribulation of those days, then you shall see the Son of Man coming in the air." Matthew 24: 29

Be Not Deceived

Let no man deceive you
Don't let them take your crown

For the enemy is busy he is traveling all around
Seeking to destroy everyone, both old and young

His ways are very crafty, he has taken many crowns.
Some that work for him are high and mighty, even renown.

They can twist the word of God to make it what its not
Causing some to lose their faith, and for eternity be lost

They set traps and stumbling blocks in the saints' paths
And if those don't get you he shoots his fiery darts.

Some will have us to believe the solution is in the praise
But, Jesus example to the end was to bend His knees and pray.

Now that a wonder legacy for every saint today
The answer is not in the praise, but faith in God when we pray.

Let no man deceive you, He taught.
Warning every believer that the spirit of deception is still at work.

"And he said, take heed that ye be not deceived. For many shall come in my name, saying, I am Christ, and the time draweth near, go ye not therefore after them." Luke 21: 8

A Deceitful Heart

Do you know what your heart is capable of?
Do you believe that your heart is only for emotions that are soft?

Do you know where all your devious plans begin?
It's in the heart of every human being.

Before an act is ever committed.
In the heart is where it is cultivated.

There it is nurtured until it is fully-grown.
Then the heart acts like it has a mind of its own.

Craving what it long to acquire
The heart becomes desperately wicked and on fire.

Deceiving the wisest and strongest of men
The heart often wins time and time again

So guard your heart with all care
For a deceitful heart is as a spear.

"The heart is deceitful above all things, and desperately wicked, who can know it?" Jeremiah 17: 9

CHAPTER VI

WE WILL STAND

- THE RACE
- WHY WE SUFFER
- LORD MAKE ME REAL
- GREEN GRASS
- THIS IS WAR

The Race

The world was at the starting line
Gathered together was all mankind

Tightly bunch they crouch ready to run.
Awaiting the signal from the gun.

Then off they ran at the gunshot
Some will finish and some will not

The course is long with many traps
You have to be prayerful or it will stop you in your tracks

Some thought they were wise but could not stay
As the course went through the valley they stop to play.

Others were complaining about the course and murmuring
Because the race was winding through the mountains

Then a few stop to take in the scenery
Because the view of the valley was a beautiful sight to see

I can hear my flesh pleading for me to quit.
But the Spirit of Lord kept saying stick with it.

So what, if there is another hill around the next turn
Soon this race will be over and I will be home.

"Wherefore seeing we are compassed about with so great a cloud of witnesses, let us lay aside every weight, and the sin which doeth so easily beset us, and let us run with patience the race that is set before us." Hebrews 12: 1

Why we suffer?

Is it because we have done wrong?
That we struggle to overcome.

Did God purpose this for our life?
Or is this the penalty of a sinner plight?

Was this passed on everyone?
The good, the bad, the weak and the strong

What's the purpose in suffering?
Is it for us to depend on Him?

Or is this a test of our faith?
To make us consider, ponder and wait

Whatever the reason why we suffer
It is my prayer it soon be over.

"But the God of all grace, who hath called us unto his eternal glory by Christ Jesus, after that ye have suffer a while, make you perfect, stablished, strengthen, settle you." 1Peter 5: 10

LORD MAKE ME REAL

Lord make me real
This is my prayer I plead

Real when I pray
Real all this day, and in every way

First make real and true to my self
So I can be real and true to everyone else

Make me real in the sanctuary
That I can give true worship and glory

Make me real with all those I meet
That in me they will find no deceit

Make me real in my heart and mind
That I will be the same throughout time

Lord just make me real through and through
For I know no hypocrite can ever please you

"He also shall be my salvation: for an hypocrite shall not come before him." Job 13: 16

Green Grass

It's a proverbial saying, "the grass is greener on the other side."
Is this true or is this an illusion born from the tears in my eyes?

I gave up my situation and now my heart is dying
I am perplexed. I wondered is life worth living?

Everything seems to go wrong
I am discouraged I felt beat down

I just want to run and get away
I believed things would be better if I don't stay

I wish things were better
On the other side of the fence everything looks greener

Perhaps I can cultivate my own
If I spend less time focusing on what is wrong

Then my situation would turn around
And the proverbial green grass would be my own.

"Be not deceived God is not mocked, for whatsoever a man soweth, that shall he also reap." Galatians 6: 7

THIS IS WAR

Saints the kingdom of God is at war
At war with our archenemy Lucifer
His campaign is to eradicate every child of God
This is foretold in the word

He has increased the intensity of the attacks
Determined to break the saints back
His instructions to his devilish host
Hit them hard where it hurts the most

Their numbers he has increased
To destroy every royal seed
Take no prisoners is his command
Destroy the young, the old, especially the preacher man

Divide families and churches bust them up
Let confusion and conflict reign from the bottom to the top
Wear them out don't give them no rest
Keep the pressure on they will break with the stress

Afflict their bodies with sickness and pain
And they will forsake their God time and time again
Whatever you do keep them off their knees
Don't let them fast and pray please

For their are a few that are fighting back
They refuse to surrender to our attack
Submitting themselves to God
They resist with the Word

For prayer and fasting is their way
These pull down our strong hold everyday
I said let them shout and let them praise
But, whatever you do, don't let them fast and pray.

"For though we walk in the flesh we do not war after the flesh. For the weapons of our warfare are not carnal, but mighty through God to the pulling down of strongholds. Casting down imaginations, and every high thing that exalteth itself against the knowledge of God, and bringing into captivity every thought to the obedience of Christ." 1Corinthians 10: 3-5

CHAPTER VII

I AM GETTING BETTER

- FORGIVE
- RECONCILIATION IS GOD'S PLAN
- WATCH YOUR WORDS
- I CAN CHANGE
- WATCH WHAT YOU THINK
- PRAY

Forgive

My brothers and sisters forgive.
Do yourself a favor and live
Hold no grudges against another
Learn to forgive my sisters and brothers

It is not okay if it is a stranger
Forgive, you may have to account for it later
Forgiving and forgiveness are good for us
They promote healing as we release the stuff

Freeing us from anger pain and guilt
As peace and joy are restored again
So forgive friends and family too
And heal the wounds that were inflicted on you

You are not responsible for what they say or do
Only for what you did or did not do
So forgive others and God will forgive you
And you will have peace in this life and the next one too.

"For if ye forgive men their trepasses, your heavenly Father will also forgive you. But if you forgive not men their trespasses, neither will your Father forgive your trespasses."
Matthew 6: 14-15

Reconciliation is God's plan

Offenses in the land
Strife among men
Some don't understand
That this is not God's plan

They what he did was wrong
He taught and preached as if he was strong
And in their presence he was sat down
Hurt and rejected the brother was gone

Then Jesus found him and healed his wounds
And commanded him to return to his own
Forgive him they say and love him we must
But too reconciled with him is asking too much

I forgive him they say, but he does not have to be my friend
And I definitely don't want him near me again
I am not bitter please understand
We don't want the brother inflicting any more pain

I know Jesus forgave and reconciled us
Forgive seventy times seven is what he commanded the church
For through his death and resurrection he reconciled me
And so with God I'll be for eternity

So holy I must live and righteous I must be
And forgive and reconcile others as Jesus did for me
For reconciliation was God's plan from the beginning
And it's his plan even as time is ending

Humbly I became obedient to God
And reconciled my brother according to the word
Then the Spirit of the Lord brought peace and harmony
Now my brother and I are worshipping God in unity

"And all things are of God, who hath reconciled us to himself by Jesus Christ, and hath given to us the ministry of reconciliation. To wit, that God was in Christ, reconciling the world to himself, not imputing their trespasses unto them, and hath committed unto us the word of reconciliation." II Corinthians 5: 18-19

Watch Your Words

Words like the spirit can give life
Words can be used wrongly as well as right
Words can bring peace or initiate a fight
Words can bring one out of darkness into light

There is a word of exhortation for the people of God
There is a word of salvation for all abroad
There is a faithful and sound word for the saints today
And a word of truth and sobriety to anchor us on this way

There are acceptable and gracious words for the discouraged
There is a word in due season that encourages
There is the word of the Lord, which is in the entire world
And His word is pure to every soul

There is a word well spoken that is like a nugget of gold
It is a good word and it comes from the Lord
There are words of wisdom to light our way
And words of knowledge to help handle every day

There is the word of Christ that should be in every heart
And the word of comfort to help us with the past
So words like the spirit can give life
And words that are pleasant are a delight

"For in many things we offend all. If any man offend not in word, the same is a perfect man, and able also to bridle the whole body." James 3: 2

I CAN CHANGE

I can change
From a homosexual to a heterosexual
From drug addiction to Christ's redemption
From a pervert to a new birth
Yes, I can change.

I can change
From a thief to giving relief
From a deceiver to a restorer
From a murderer to a life giver
I can change

I can change
From a trickster and a liar to a devil chaser
From a fornicator to the Lord's speaker
From a loser to a winner
Yes I can change

I can change
From prostitution to God's family plan
From an abuser to a lover
From a sinner to a believer
I can change

I can change
I can turn defeat into victory
Poverty into prosperity
Fear into faith
Yes I can change

I can change
From being weak to being strong
To being right from being wrong
From darkness to light
I can and I am, changed!

"I can do all things through Christ which strengtheneth me."
Philippians 4: 13

WATCH WHAT YOU THINK

No more will I think on things that are bad
Things that are sad are untrue
For in these things there are no praise or virtue
And it does not help you or me

Therefore I will meditate on things that are honest
And I will feast on things that are just
For in these things are virtue and praise
Cause they testify of God saving grace

I will think on those things that are lovely
I will meditate on things that are pure
For in these things are praise and virtue
And in these things we can praise God for sure

"For as he thinketh in his heart, so is he." Proverb 23: 7

Pray

It is often repeated that prayer changes things
Pray, they say to God who can do anything

Pray in the morning to start your day
Pray prayers of thanksgiving, for his protection along the way

Pray for our world leaders and all in authority
Pray that God touch their hearts and give integrity

Pray for our neighborhoods, communities, and cities too
Pray for peace everywhere in countries far and close to you

Pray for healing in the land
Pray for man to understand God's divine plan

Pray for the ungodly and sinners always
Pray that God will have mercy and they will be saved

Pray when everything is going well
Pray on those days when you are going through hell

Pray God's will be done in the earth
Pray that you are the vessel He uses, for there is hope

"I will therefore that men pray everywhere, lifting up holy hands, without wrath and doubting." I Timothy 2: 8

CHAPTER VIII

BUILDING EACH OTHER

- I BELIEVE IN YOU
- INSPIRATORS
- HE IS WITH YOU
- MY CHILD
- YOU BELIEVE IN ME

I BELIEVE IN YOU

I see your beauty deep inside, and the very fabrics that build your character.
I see your strength and confidence rising above the inward dissidence.

I believe in you; courage and fortitude reside within you.
You are no stranger to struggle, opposition or fear.
Though haunted by past experiences, heartaches and tears.

I believe in you, and deep in you something wonderful is taking shape.
The storms of life will not break it they came to help shape you within it.

Hold your head up, put a smile on face.
It is the enemy desire for you to quit in disgrace.
Nevertheless, I am confident, that deep within you lies untapped strength.

So even though your energy may seem spent.
I believe in you, and you shall rise again.

"But they that wait upon the Lord shall renew their strength; they shall mount up with wings as eagles, they shall run, and not be weary, and they shall walk, and not faint." Isaiah 40: 28-31

Inspirators

You inspired me to desire, aspire, acquire, to dream.
You are the inspirators of my life, edifying and perfecting
Constantly molding and shaping me with your visions.

How can I protest or regress from these men and women that
trouble me.
They demand of me to desire, to aspire, acquire, to dream.

From my infancy to adulthood these have profoundly impacted
my life.
Imparting their wisdom and vision within me of a better life.

And what you see today are the results of seeds sown during
those forgotten yesterdays.
Hence my future is not determined by what I am today,
But by the wonderful things my inspirators imparted day by day.

So quite naturally, I am an inspirator and it's quite challenging I
deem.
Helping others desire, aspire, acquire and dream.

"The Lord God had given me the tongue of the learned, that I should know how to speak a word in season to him that is weary; he wakeneth morning by morning, he wakeneth my ear to hear as the learned. The Lord God had opened my ear, and I was not rebellious, neither turned away back." Isaiah 50: 4 - 5

HE IS WITH YOU

Sometimes in times of trouble, it seems the Lord is not with you.
You cannot seem to find Him and your prayers are not getting
through.

You have read your Bible and fasted, praised and worship too.
Lord you say, "come now, can you not see I am going through?'

You know He delivered Daniel out of the lions' den
And the children across the Red Sea,
But in your mind you wonder, Lord can you work this out for
me?

So remember when you are going through, that God's word is
written just for you.
Just wait on him, He is sure to bring you through.

"Many are the afflictions of the righteous: but the Lord delivered him from it all." Psalm 34: 19

My Child

Having you taught me a little more about life.
I was selfish, self-centered, and concerned only about the bright
lights.

I wanted to abort, but I thought long and hard
Concerning the right for life, and the reasons to abort came short.

You came amidst mixed emotions, the joy of having you and the
despair.
What am I going to do and how in the world am I going to
prepare?

Suddenly my life has changed I am no longer the same,
I am a mother and you are my child

Just look at you, come on smile for mammy
That right, smile everything will be all right.

With the help of the Lord, family and friends we shall do fine.
And I pledge to you that I will be there for you, with my love,
support, and my time.

I will not abuse, misuse, or neglect you neither will I abandon
you for any cause.
My child I pledge always to love and to inspire you, and guide
you on the right course.

"Lo, children are an heritage of the Lord; and the fruit of the womb is his reward." Psalm 127: 3

YOU BELIEVE IN ME

I was troubled looking for my place,

Had no direction just an empty look on my face.

Did not know where I was heading or what my life was about.

I needed direction but there was so much doubt.

I did not have the strength or the confidence to believe in me.

A world of confusion and turmoil was all I was able to conceive.

When family and friends were in doubt, you believed in me.

You inspired, supported, and gave me courage to proceed

How could I perceive the things you spoke of, that lay within.

Nor did I understand that destiny had drawn us together, to bring me to this end.

Because of you my life has changed.

And now I am confident, that it will never be the same.

"Now unto him that is able to keep you from falling, and to present you faultless before the presence of his glory with exceeding joy, to the only wise God our Savior, be glory and majesty, dominion and power, both now and ever." Jude 24 - 25

CHAPTER IX

BLESSED ASSURANCE

- JESUS COMFORTS
- THE LAST SHALL BE FIRST
- HIS GLORY
- I BELIEVE GOD

Jesus Comforts

Comfort, comfort my people
Said the Lord God Almighty

My friend I see your agony
Pain and hurt was part of my life story

Allow me to share my testimony
Perhaps you can be strengthen through me

I was broken and in despair
Often feeling no one card

Tossed to an fro by my imagination
And manipulated by my situations

I did not know which way to turn
The truth is I was tired of being burned

I had lost my faith and confidence
From relying too much on men

Then entered Jesus Christ my King
And in Him my faith was renewed again

He assured me and gave me peace
His comfort was my sweet relief

I never could have found a sweeter friend
That stuck with me to the very end.

"Now our Lord Jesus Christ himself, and God, even our Father, which hath loved us, and hath given us everlasting consolation and good hope through grace, comfort your hearts, and establish you in every good word and work." II Thessalonians 2: 16 - 17

THE LAST SHALL BE FIRST

Ever since the beginning of time
God honored and blessed the first in line

He blessed the first-born above his brethren
But every so often God changed the system

He changed it when He said, "the elder shall serve the younger"
And Isaac blessed Jacob with the blessing meant for Esau

Then Israel blessed Joseph 's two sons
And the blessing for the elder was given to the younger one

Jacob confirmed what God had begun with him
For this was the beginning of a new thing

Who could believe that the first would be last?
As Abraham and Joseph we also would be flabbergast

Then God sent Samuel to anoint a king
And the first was rejected and the last was anointed over him

Thus when Jesus came
He used parables to make this point plain

That the last would be first and the first last
Changing the way it was done in the past.

"So the last shall be first, and the first last. For many be called, but few chosen." Matthew 20: 16

His Glory

Lord I want to be in the midst of your Glory
When your Glory comes in the sanctuary

Prepare me I want to be ready
When your Glory descends on me

I want to feel the freshness that it brings
When your Glory comes in as the wind

In your presence I will drink
And satisfy the longing that's within

Fill me Savior fill me
Fill every crevice of my being

Let my soul be saturated with your Glory
Even as the fields are satisfy with the rain

Let your Glory radiates from your presence
And refresh my soul all over again

"Lift up your head O ye gates and be ye lift up ye everlasting doors, and the King of Glory shall come in." Psalm 24: 7

I BELIEVE GOD

Who do you believe when God speaks?
Is it your reasoning or your friend down the street?

How do you know He is talking to you?
Is it because your friends confirms it is true

What do you say to those that differ with you?
I believe God and know Him to be true

What do you do when your faith is tested and tried?
Do you get angry, frustrated and cry?

What makes you put up with the criticism and skeptics?
Is it because you believe God and rest in His assurances?

What gives you this confidence and faith in God?
I believe God and obey His word

"Wherefore, sirs, be of good cheer, for I believe God, that it shall be even as it was told me." Acts 27: 25

CHAPTER X

HELPING HANDS

- A CHAMPION FOR THE MASSES
- GIVE
- PRAYER PARTNERS
- I OWE YOU

A Champion for the Masses

You are a woman of color, a woman of class.

A woman with a heart, that's a champion for the mass.

Addressing the issues that concern all people.

You bring to light information that is timely and sensible.

Woman you are a champion for everyone cause

For direction and inspiration, you are a source

You recognize and inspire many, to rise above life circumstances

Appreciating and rewarding those that overcome their hindrances

Touching lives and giving hope

You entice many, back from the proverbial "end of the rope."

Although I commend you I know you do not need my praise

As I look around woman, your works are praising you in every
place.

"For if thou altogether hold thy peace at this time, then shall enlargement and deliverance arise to the Jews from another place." Esther 4: 14

GIVE

Give and it shall be given unto you
Give to your friends and enemies too
Give people as Jesus did
He gave His life that we might live

Give to those that cannot pay you back
Expecting nothing in return for that
Give to the poor and you shall not lack
Give of your substance as seeds in a sack

Give to the widows and fatherless too
Remember what God commanded us to do
Give to each other your time
As you lend a helping hand

Give and it shall be given back to you
This is what Christ desires us to do
Give and do it cheerfully
That's the word from God, through me.

"I have showed you all things, how that so laboring ye ought to support the weak, and to remember the words of the Lord Jesus, how he said, it is more blessed to give than to receive."
Acts 20: 35

Prayer Partners

To those God fearing people travailing that I might stand
God knew I needed help until I understand

He blessed me with you, for it took your prayer to see me through
Each of you were significant in preparing me for the next stage

You were chosen of God to assist me in fulfilling His course
And you carried out your assignment without using any force

Demonstrating that prayer to God is the answer
While you waited on God at the altar

And when the days seem dark and the nights long
I thank God for the Comforter

These have played a significant part
Birthing, imparting, and equipping me for the master

And though the enemy laid traps and snares
God revealed the enemy plans, and turned them into disaster

This is my testimony to you
I thank God for my prayer partners praying me through

"Confess your faults one to another, and pray one for another, that you might be healed." James 5: 16

I OWE YOU

My friend I owe you a lot of things
Some significant while others are not
Some things I owe are tangible
Others I cannot see, or just forgot

Some things I owe one day I will repay
Others I will never be able to, I'm sorry to say
I owe you big time, I must agree
Some money, some stuff, hmmm.... Let me see

Perhaps, I owe you all of me
How can I repay, I wonder when I owe you so much
Have you considered giving me the stuff?
Then all I will owe you is for this one favor, oh nooo...

I still owe you big time
And I don't have a dime
I'll talk to you later
Right now, I need a savior

"Owe no man anything, but to love one another; for he that loveth another had fulfilled the law." Romans 13: 8

Chapter XI

All in a Day

- We are Different
- Tell the Truth about Christmas
- I am a Christian
- Laughter
- Death
- I have a Home in Glory

We are Different

We are different, you must agree
And have differences like everybody

So what if we are different
For friends our differences are life's challenges

You are difference that not hard to see?
But with our differences you are just like me

You are a different color and nationality
And our culture is different from this society

We were raised to believe this and that
So what! Let's be different and learn to adapt

What you do not change, I will learn to accept
And with our differences, there must be respect

Now that we are closer than we have ever been
We are no difference from each other, as it once seemed

"A man that hath friends must shew himself friendly; and there is a friend that sticks closer than a brother." Proverb 18: 24

Tell the Truth about Christmas

Tell the truth about Christmas
How Jesus Christ was born
Tell the truth about Christmas
Santa the Clown the does not belong

Tell the world the truth
Why we celebrate Christ's birth
How He represented hope
To men dying on earth

Then the enemy gave a substitute
And introduced Santa and his reindeers
To distract us from the birth of the Savior
He gave us a masquerader

Santa does not own a kingdom
Not even a country town
He masquerades as a king
Even though he possesses nothing

He acts like he can satisfy our every whim
And through time, he has made himself a king
Deceiving the unknowing with his lies about his wealth
He tries to steal the glory that belongs to the Son of God himself

So tell the truth why we celebrate Christmas
Tell the truth that there is no Santa the Clown
Tell the truth about Christ's birth
And the life He lived on the earth

"For unto us is born this day in the city of David, a Savior, which is Christ the Lord." Luke 2: 11

I AM A CHRISTIAN

Did you say be a Christian, you me? I replied.
Being a Christian is dull and boring and way too easy.
I thought there was no challenges.
Just the same rudimentary stuff

I never thought if I read the Bible
I would learn about His promises and find them quite enough.
What He did for others He promised to do for me
If I will have faith and trust Him totally

How could I have known the excitement?
That's a part of living holy.
Challenged everyday to live a righteous life
Depending on Jesus only.

How I wish I had known my Savior sooner
And given my life to him.
When I think of all the wrongs I have done
And the ungodly things I did.

For I thought being a Christian was too easy
Until I submitted my life to Him
Then I learned excitement comes from pleasing my Savior
Jesus Christ the risen King

You see I was once a sinner
And faithfully I served my flesh
But thank God, Now I am a Christian;
And I am serving Jesus Christ the very best

"Therefore if any man be in Christ, he is a new creature: old things are passed away; behold all things are become new." II Cor. 5: 17

LAUGHTER

Laughter is like medicine, it does everybody good.

It works so incredibly that it can change an ugly mood.

It can be contagious, causing others to laugh throughout
the day.

It will lift a heavy heart, and keep the heartaches at bay.

Laughter brings friends closer together,

And makes you smile long after they have gone their way.

So remember when you are feeling sad just laugh.

For laughter makes a dreary day seem so bright and clear.

So as your inspirational doctor, this is what my prescription
says,

Have a good laugh at least three times a day.

"A merry heart doeth good like a medicine." Proverb 17: 22

Death

What is it about death?
That cause so many to be upset
A loved one dying
Folks can't sleep they are crying

When a loved one crosses over into eternity street
You just can imagine the family lost and feelings of grief
Whether they were a saint or a sinner
The death of a loved one makes us all stop and ponder

Some may wonder where did they go?
Are they above or somewhere below?
Then there is the numbness and void that last for a while
And the longing and helplessness that makes you cry

Life seems so empty without our loved one here
This is a sign that we missed them and wish they were there
Their death was a blow that left our energy spent
Now learning to lives requires some strength

I am taking the time to prepare my soul
For one day upon me death will hold
I want to be ready when he comes for me
That all may rejoice when I leave this body

"But I would not have you to be ignorant, brethren, concerning them which are dead, that ye sorrow not, even as others which had no hope." I Thessalonians 4: 13

I HAVE A HOME IN GLORY

Don't weep over my body
I am not here I am at home glory
I have lived the time God gave me
Did my best to used it wisely

Because I knew I had a home in glory

This body of mine been on the earth for some time
Has experienced sunshine, rain, joy and pain
I was once beautiful, young, strong, and supple
Since has grown old, weak and feeble

As I waited on my trip home to glory

At an early age my life to Christ I gave
Knowing through His death and resurrection I will live
I knew one day I was going to leave this place
Leave family and friends their smiles and warm embrace

Finally, I am on my journey home to glory

I had no regrets when I took my leave
And don't you weep rejoice with me
I am in the place that I have always longed to be
What a place! No night, no pain, no agony

You'll see me in my new home if you get to glory

"For we know that if our earthly house of this tabernacle were dissolved, we have a building of God, an house not made with hands, eternal in the heavens." II Cor. 5: 1

About the Author

David Jacque was born on the island of Trinidad & Tobago. He is a husband, father, and an ordained Elder in the Church of God in Christ. This anointed teacher ministers under the inspiration of the Holy Ghost.

This former track star is a poet, and the author of several other books. He writes under the inspiration of the Holy Spirit, addressing the issues of life. He resides in Lansing, Michigan and attends New Hope Church of God in Christ.

To contact the author, write:

David Jacque
P O Box 618
Dimondale, Michigan 48821
Email: ministerjd@yahoo.com

Published by:

Cyberlab Ministry Publishing
Post Office Box
Dimondale, Michigan 48821
Cyberlabministry@yahoo.com